Explaining Repentance

Ed Roebert

Sovereign World

British Library Cataloguing in Publication Data
Roebert, Edmund
Explaining Repentance
1. Salvation
2. Title
234.5

ISBN: 1 85240 067 6

This Sovereign World book is distributed in North America by Renew Books,
a ministry of Gospel Light, Ventura, California, USA. For a free catalog of resources
from Renew Books/Gospel Light, please contact your Christian supplier
or call 1-800-4-GOSPEL.

SOVEREIGN WORLD LIMITED
P.O. Box 777, Tonbridge, Kent TN11 0ZS, England.

Typeset and printed in the UK by Sussex Litho Ltd, Chichester, West Sussex.

Contents

Preface   4

Introduction   5

1   Six Foundation Stones   7

2   The Meaning Of Repentance   11

3   The Need For Repentance   13

4   The Call To Repentance   19

5   The Nature Of Repentance   23

6   The Reactions To Repentance   27

7   The Mechanics Of Repentance   39

8   The Ramifications Of Repentance   43

9   The Christian And Repentance   47

10 Personal Application   49

11 The Steps Into Repentance   51

Preface

This booklet is part of a *series* designed to help you grow to maturity in Christ. Many new converts who long to make progress in their Christian lives struggle with the *how* of the process. This booklet is designed to help you take the first steps along the road.

I have had the privilege of pastoring a church for the past twenty years and am fully aware of the difficulties people encounter in their spiritual growth. Recently I was introduced to Leroy Eim's book, *The Lost Art of Disciple Making*. I found this book very helpful, especially the overall pattern he suggests for leading a person to maturity.

Once a person meets Jesus and is born again he becomes

A convert. As certain principles from the Word of God are built into his life, he becomes

A disciple. As a disciple he is trained in *how* to serve the Lord and is thus equipped to become

A worker. It's a privilege to serve the Lord, but as one continues to serve Him the whole matter of leadership soon emerges. As a person is trained in the principles of leadership he should emerge as

A leader. The Lord always works through leadership and is therefore looking for mature leaders.

Introduction

The Bible places great emphasis on the subject of repentance. It is listed as the first of the foundation doctrines in Hebrews:

> *The first principles of the oracles of God...repentance from dead works.* (Hebrews 5:12; 6:1)

It was the message that John the Baptist preached as he said:

> *Repent, for the kingdom of heaven is at hand.*
> (Matthew 3:2)

It was the message that Jesus preached at the time of the launching of his ministry.

> *From that time Jesus began to preach and to say: 'Repent, for the kingdom of heaven is at hand'.*
> (Matthew 4:17)

On the Day of Pentecost, as the church was launched in power, Peter preached the same message under the anointing of the Holy Spirit, in response to the question: 'Men and brethren, what shall we do?'

> *Then Peter said unto them, Repent and be baptised every*

one of you, in the name of Jesus Christ, for the remission
of sins . . .   (Acts 2:38)

This message was echoed by the early church as Paul preached to the unconverted religious people of his day, and said:

and the times of this ignorance God overlooked, but
now commands all men everywhere to repent, because
he has appointed a day, in which he will judge the world
in righteousness.   (Acts 17:30)

Have you ever come to God in repentance? If not, then you have not even laid the first foundation stone of the Christian life.

1

Six Foundation Stones

The Bible states that there are six foundation stones upon which we must build our lives, and upon which the church must be built. If your life is not built upon this solid foundation, you will need to change your life and begin to build on these solid foundation stones. If your church is not built on these foundation stones, look around for a church that is, and join it.

> *Therefore, leaving the principles of the doctrine of Christ, let us go on unto perfection, not laying again the foundation of repentance from dead works and of faith towards God; of the doctrine of baptisms, and laying on of hands, and of resurrection of the dead, and of eternal judgement.* (Hebrews 6:1–3)

It is tragically true that all six of these doctrines have been neglected, twisted or rejected by many. Think about it for a moment!

Repentance

Repentance has by many been replaced by the 'Come to Jesus' teaching. The fact is that you cannot come without repentance.

Faith towards God

This has been changed to faith in ourselves, faith in our churches, faith in our creeds. Even Christians who have taken the initial step in their life of faith, seem to live their subsequent lives without much faith.

Be honest—how much faith does it take you to live your kind of Christian life?

Doctrine of baptisms

The church has mutilated this doctrine. If there has ever been a subject the church has fought over, it's been the subject of the believer's baptism versus infant baptism.

This has been a trick of the devil to rob us of a solid foundation. Then, too, the baptism of the Holy Spirit has been a hotly disputed subject. In some circles, when it is raised, sparks fly!

The laying on of hands

This doctrine has been largely dropped from the agenda. Many churches have virtually practised this only at the ordination of a man to the ministry.

So much blessing, so much health and healing, so much release of power, so many gifts and ministries have not been imparted because this doctrine has been neglected.

Resurrection of the dead

Many have denied the resurrection of Jesus. Others have rejected the resurrection of our bodies on resurrection day.

Most have not gone on to experience the resurrection life of Jesus as a daily experience.

Eternal judgement

Many have simply rejected the clear statement of scripture in favour of their soppy view of a 'loving God'.

Others have substituted a place of refining as a stepping stone to heaven. But God still says there is an eternal judgement. Be sure to get six solid foundation blocks under your feet—under your church.

2

The Meaning Of Repentance

In order to be built on the solid foundation of repentance we need to consider its true meaning. The word means more than being sorry for what one has done, although this always accompanies real repentance. It also means more than to stop sinning, although every repentant person will deliberately stop sinning. In essence, repentance is a right about turn involving part of a person, their mind, their emotions, and their will. It is a total change of life, a total change of direction, it is becoming a totally new person.

The Greek word for repentance is *metanoia*. This compound word is comprised of two parts, 'meta' meaning 'after'—implying change, and 'noia' coming from the word *nous*, 'mind'. So repentance is 'a change of mind (after)'—after hearing the Word and being touched by the Holy Spirit.

Being sorrowful for sins leads to repentance. You can have sorrow that does not lead to repentance. A person can be outwardly sorrowful because they have been caught in the act of sin, and yet never turn from it.

Now I rejoice, not that ye were made sorry but that you sorrowed to repentance: for ye were made sorry after a godly manner, that ye might receive damage by us in nothing. For godly sorrow worketh repentance to salvation not to be repented of [or regretted—this is a dif-

*ferent Greek word] but the sorrow of this world worketh
death.*   (2 Corinthians 7:9–10)

Repentance involves a change in conduct. This should be
evidenced by restitution (putting wrong things right). See
what Zacchaeus did:

> *And Zacchaeus stood and said unto the Lord, Behold,
> Lord, the half of my goods I give to the poor; if I have
> taken anything from any man by false accusation [cheat-
> ing] I restore him fourfold.* [This was according to Jew-
> ish law, Exodus 22:1. See also Numbers 5:17.] *And
> Jesus said unto him, This day is salvation come to this
> house...*   (Luke 19:8,9)

What a change in his conduct! Evidence of a deep change
of mind and heart. This is repentance.

3

The Need For Repentance

When God created man on the sixth day of creation we are told:

> *So God created man in his own image, in the image of God created he him.* (Genesis 1:27)

At the end of this sixth day of creating, we are told:

> *And God saw everything he had made and behold it was very good.* (Genesis 1:31a)

Obviously God created man perfect. He placed man in the perfect garden of Eden and gave him dominion (Genesis 1:28). But God placed one restriction on man:

> *And the Lord God took the man, and put him into the garden of Eden, to till and to keep it.*
> *And the Lord God commanded the man saying, Of every tree in the garden thou mayest freely eat. But of the tree of the knowledge of good and evil, thou shalt not eat of it: for in the day that thou eatest thereof thou shalt surely die.* (Genesis 2:15–17)

Adam and Eve disregarded this restriction and as a result something happened to them which God equated with death. I would like to suggest that:

13

Their spirits

—that part of them created especially for fellowship with God, shrivelled up and died, or at least lapsed into a coma, and as a result their relationship with God died. *'Thou shalt surely die.'*

Their souls

—that part of them created especially for fellowship with like beings, started to degenerate as the rot of death set in. The soul includes the mind, the emotions, and the will.

With their minds in decay, no longer did they think God's way or God's thoughts, and they began to think evil. Death had set in. The rot had also set in, in their emotions. No longer did they feel as God feels, or react as God reacts. Rather, different evil emotions began to dominate them, like the emotions of hate that resulted in Cain killing his brother Abel.

Then, too, their wills became twisted, and what they wanted to do became more important than what God wanted them to do. Death had reached every part of their souls. *'Thou shalt surely die.'*

Their bodies

—especially created to enable them to relate to the physical world of substance, also came under the curse of death. As a result of their sin, their bodies commenced to decay and finally, both Adam and Eve died. *'Thou shalt surely die.'*

This curse of sin, that ultimately led to the death of Adam and Eve, has been handed down to the entire human race.

Paul makes that clear in Romans 5:12:

> *Wherefore, as by one man sin entered into the world (that is, by Adam), and death by sin, and so death passed upon all men, for all have sinned.*

This is the reason why:

> *God now commands all men everywhere to repent.*
> (Acts 17:30)

This curse of death on the human race has affected every one of us more than we realise. Not only is there an effect coming down from Adam, but this curse is further reinforced by our personal sinning.

What happens to me when I sin?

Sin blinds

> *The god of this world [Satan] has blinded the minds of them who believe not, lest the light of the glorious gospel of Christ, who is the image of God, should shine unto them.*
> (2 Corinthians 4:4)

Sin separates

> *This I say therefore, and testify in the Lord, that ye henceforth walk not as other Gentiles [heathens] walk, in the vanity of their mind, having the understanding darkened, being alienated [separated] from the life of God through the ignorance that is in them.*
> (Ephesians 4:17,18)

> *But your iniquities have separated between you and your God, and your sins have hidden his face from you, and he will not hear.*
> (Isaiah 59:2)

Sin is like a thick cloud which blots out the sun. This is why God seems miles away. He is pure and holy. He hates sin. He cannot and will not look on sin. Sin blocks the way to Him. Sin cuts us off from God in this life, and in the life to come. Be quite clear about this; hell is a grim and dreadful reality for *all* who reject Jesus Christ in this life.

Sin corrupts the conscience
Paul, writing to Titus, says:

> *Unto the pure all things are pure, but unto them that are defiled and unbelieving is nothing pure; but even their mind and conscience is defiled.* (Titus 1:15)

This means that the conscience of an unbeliever is unreliable, for it has been defiled. He may feel that his conscience is alert and accurate, but God says it is defiled. This should alarm each one of us. Paul writes to Timothy and speaks about people whose consciences have been seared (branded—burned) with a hot iron.

With a conscience that is warped and scarred and defiled, it is possible to believe that right is wrong and wrong is right. That is why we need to repent.

Sin corrupts the will
The fall of man resulted in the corruption and the perversion of the will. The will is the control room of man. The Bible tells us:

> *All we like sheep have gone astray. We have turned every one to his own way.* (Isaiah 53:6)

The unrepentant will is stubborn, rebellious and unbending. That is why we need to repent!

16

Sin spreads

Sin is like weeds in a garden—if not rooted out, they will soon overrun it. Little acts of dishonesty and disobedience soon become habits we cannot break. The Bible says:

> Know ye not that to whom ye yield yourselves servants to obey, his servant ye are to whom ye obey, whether of sin unto death, or obedience unto righteousness.
>
> (Romans 6:16)

Lying once opens the way to becoming enslaved to lying. Allowing your mind to wander lustfully leads to lust controlling your mind. This process must be stopped before you are controlled. This is why we need to repent!

Scripture therefore clearly shows that:

Sin blinds the mind
Sin separates from God
Sin corrupts the conscience
Sin corrupts the will
Sin spreads into habits.

That is why God emphasises the need for repentance.

Sin makes God angry

> The wrath of God is revealed from heaven against all ungodliness and unrighteousness of men, who hold the truth in unrighteousness [who suppress the truth by their wickedness].   (Romans 1:18 NIV)

> God judgeth the righteous, and God is angry with the wicked every day.   (Psalm 7:11)

The need for repentance should always be emphasised.

Against the backdrop of man's critical position, man's desperate situation, down through the history of time God has faithfully been calling men and women to repent.

4

The Call To Repentance

In the Old Testament God's messengers call on the people to turn; in the New Testament they call on the people to repent.

In the Old Testament

Early in their history the Lord God taught His people to turn to Him.

> But if from there thou shalt seek the Lord thy God, thou shalt find him, if thou seek him with all thy heart and with all thy soul.

> When thou art in tribulation, and all these things are come upon thee, even in the latter days, if thou turn to the Lord thy God, and shalt be obedient unto his voice; (for the Lord thy God is a merciful God;) he will not forsake thee... (Deuteronomy 4:29–31)

The prophet Isaiah preached the same message:

> And the Redeemer shall come to Zion, and unto those who turn from transgression in Jacob, saith the Lord. (Isaiah 59:20)

Hear the call of Jeremiah, the weeping prophet:

> *Go and proclaim these words toward the north and say,*
> *return thou backsliding Israel, saith the Lord; and I will*
> *not cause my anger to fall on you....*
>
> *Turn, O backsliding children, saith the Lord; for I am*
> *married to you.* (Jeremiah 3:12,14)

The prophet Ezekiel echoed the same message:

> *Repent, and turn yourselves from all your transgres-*
> *sions; so iniquity shall not be your ruin.*
>
> (Ezekiel 18:30b)

Hosea brings the same message:

> *But you must return to your God, maintain love and*
> *justice, and wait for your God always.* (Hosea 12:6 NIV)

In like vein Zechariah the prophet says:

> *Therefore, say unto them, Thus saith the Lord of hosts,*
> *turn ye unto me saith the Lord of hosts, and I will turn*
> *unto you, saith the Lord of hosts.* (Zechariah 1:3)

Turn! is the clear message of the Old Testament.

In the New Testament

Jesus said:

> *Repent for the kingdom of heaven is at hand.*
>
> (Matthew 4:17)
>
> *Woe unto thee, Chorazin! Woe unto thee, Bethsaida!*

20

For if the mighty works, which were done in you, had been done in Tyre and Sidon, they would have repented long ago in sackcloth and ashes. (Matthew 11:21)

The time is fulfilled, and the kingdom of God is at hand; Repent ye, and believe the gospel. (Mark 1:15)

I tell you, Nay: but, except ye repent, ye shall all likewise perish. (Luke 13:3,5)

I say unto you, that likewise joy shall be in heaven over one sinner that repenteth, more than over ninety and nine just persons, which need no repentance.
(Luke 15:7)

The early Christians

Went out, and preached that men should repent.
(Mark 6:12)

Down through the years they continued to preach and teach their message.

Repent and be baptised every one of you. (Acts 2:38)

Repent ye therefore, and be converted, that your sins may be blotted out. (Acts 3:19)

Repent therefore of this thy wickedness, and pray God, if perhaps the thought of thine heart may be forgiven thee.
(Acts 8:22)

The times of this ignorance God overlooked, but now commandeth all men everywhere to repent. (Acts 17:30)

Whereupon, O king Agrippa, I was not disobedient unto the heavenly vision. But showed first unto them of Damascus, and at Jerusalem, and throughout all the coasts of Judaea, and then to the Gentiles, that they should repent and turn to God, and do works meet for repentance. (Acts 26:19,20)

The book of the Revelation endorses this message

Remember therefore from whence thou art fallen, and repent, and do the first works; or else I will come unto thee quickly, and will remove thy candlestick [lampstand, NIV] out of his place, except thou repent.
(Revelation 2:5)

Repent or else I will come unto thee quickly, and will fight against them with the sword of my mouth.
(Revelation 2:16)

And I gave her space to repent of her fornication, and she repented not. (Revelation 2:21)

As many as I love, I rebuke and chasten, be zealous therefore, and repent. (Revelation 3:19)

Not all have, nor will all repent!

And the rest of the men who were not killed by these plagues yet repented not... (Revelation 9:20)

And men were scorched with great heat, and blasphemed the name of God, which had power over these plagues; and they repented not to give him glory.
(Revelation 16:9)

So consistently, both in the Old and New Testaments, the loving call of God goes out, calling all men everywhere to repent.

5

The Nature Of Repentance

For all who respond positively to the call of the Lord to repentance, there needs to be a clear understanding of the nature of repentance.

Confession is a stepping-stone to Repentance

It is possible to confess your sins and yet not repent, or turn your back on those sins. In the Greek of the original New Testament, we find the word for 'confession' is very descriptive. This compound word *homologeo* brings together two important facts of confession: 'homos' means 'the same' and 'logeo' means 'to say'. So confession means 'to say the same (thing)'. For example, a man may listen to an anointed preacher, and as he does, suddenly feel a twinge of guilt— it's as if the Holy Spirit quietly whispers to him, 'Your life is not right with God.'

At that point the man has two options. He can reject what he is hearing, or he can accept and agree with the whisper of the Holy Spirit. Confession is saying the same thing that the Holy Spirit says about our lives. It is admitting and acknowledging that the Holy Spirit is speaking the truth about our lives. When the Holy Spirit says, 'You have lied and been dishonest', true confession says the same thing: 'Yes, Lord, I have lied and been dishonest.' It is simply a matter of agreeing with God and saying what He says.

Now it is possible to admit that you have sinned, and in so doing, confess, but that is no guarantee that you will turn your back on that sin. Confession is clearly only a stepping-stone towards repentance.

Repentance is turning from wickedness

Repentance is a change of heart towards wickedness. But, what sort of wickedness? What is wickedness? Well, the word 'wickedness', as it is used in the New Testament, has several shades of meaning. To be wicked is to be bad, evil, lawless, naughty, or it can even mean to do something amiss, or malicious, or miserable.

Peter addresses Simon the sorcerer against the backdrop of his involvements in sorcery, and his offer of money for the power to lay hands on people, that they may receive the Holy Spirit:

> *But Peter said unto him, Thy money perish with thee, because thou hast thought that the gift of God may be purchased with money. Thou hast neither part nor lot in this matter; for thy heart is not right in the sight of God. Repent, therefore, of this thy wickedness, and pray God, if perhaps the thought of thine heart may be forgiven thee.* (Acts 8:20–22)

It is not clear from the subsequent verses whether Simon repented or not. But, what is most important of all to you is, have *you* repented?

The nature of repentance is further clarified by the writer to the Hebrews. He speaks of:

Repentance from dead works

The Amplified Bible says: '*Repentance and abandonment of dead works* [dead formalism].'

The Living Bible says: '*Surely we don't need to speak further about the foolishness of trying to be saved by being good.*'

'*Dead works*' (Hebrews 6:1) are all human efforts to atone for our sins. And man has thought up so many dead works.

Barnes comments as follows:

> The reference may be either to those actions which were sinful in their nature, or to those which related to the forms of religion, where there was no spiritual life. This is the character of much of the religion of the Jews; and conversion to the true religion consisted greatly in repentance for having relied on those heartless and hollow forms. When formalists are converted, one of the first and main concerns of their minds in conversion, consists in deep and genuine sorrow for their dependence on those forms. (From Barnes on Hebrews)

The Jews relied on the fact that they were 'children of Abraham'—part of God's special nation. They also relied on the fact that they were custodians of the Scriptures, and on their ceremonies and sacrifices. None of these had the power to take away their sins. As such they were all dead works!

Today religious people rely on their 'Christian' background. Some go as far as to believe that their being sprinkled makes them covenant children. Others believe that church membership is all they need to secure them a place in heaven. Some believe that all of the above add up to make them children of God. All are *dead works*.

Repentance means turning our backs on our dependence

on these forms. We are to depend on Jesus; on His shed blood, and on His substitutionary death on the cross for us, *alone*, as being the basis for salvation. *Have you repented from all your dead works?*

In order that we may experience genuine, God-given repentance, it is important to understand that God is the author and originator of repentance. True repentance takes place only as we allow the Holy Spirit to work in our lives.

6

The Reactions To Repentance

There are many enemies of this work of the Holy Spirit in our lives, and among the chief of these is self-righteousness and self-justification.

Many people have often been stirred by the Holy Spirit to an awareness of their sin, and wrong standing before God. Instead of letting the Spirit of God bring this work to ripeness, they are relieved when the old self in them rushes to the rescue with loads and loads of self-justification. The result is that the work of the Holy Spirit is neutralised and they are thereby robbed of so many rich blessings.

Among the many reactions to the convicting work of the Holy Spirit with a view to leading us to repentance is:

1. Indifference

With a sweeping thought: 'Lord, that's not for me', or 'I shouldn't allow myself to be thinking this way', all the convicting work of the Holy Spirit is swept aside. That is the height of indifference!

Then, too, many show their indifference by saying, 'Everybody is doing that today. Why shouldn't I also be allowed to do the same?'

Why is there this indifference?
Because of a decline in moral standards world-wide.

Because so often the media makes a hero out of a wicked person. For example, it will give extra exposure to a person who has been married ten or twelve times, without commenting negatively.

Because many have not received a correct foundation in the Word of God, and in God's laws and standards.

Because few clearly understand what sin is in the sight of God.

Because few understand the message of the cross, and what Jesus had to go through to pay for our sin.

Indifference is often caused by a misunderstanding of the seriousness of sin.

These are a few of the major reasons why some people are indifferent to the call of the Holy Spirit to repent.

What is sin?
Sin is coming short of God's divine standard.

> *For all have sinned and come short of the glory of God.*
> (Romans 3:23)

It could be 10 per cent short. It could be 40 per cent short. Or 80 per cent short. The issue is not the percentage, but the fact that *all* have come short, for *all* have sinned. What implications does this have for you?

Sin is also defined as transgression of the law.

> *Whatsoever committeth [practises] sin transgresses [violates] the law, for sin is the transgression of the law.*
> (1 John 3:4)

Violate a traffic law and you sin. Violate a civil law and you sin against the government. Violate God's law and you sin against God.

Sin is failure to do what is right! James makes this clear as he says:

Therefore, to him that knoweth to do good, and doeth it not, to him it is sin. (James 4:17)

This is generally referred to as the sin of omission.

If sin is coming short of God's standard, no matter how little; if sin is violating God's law, no matter which one; and if sin is failure to do what is right, then one understands why the Bible says, '*all* have sinned.'

What does sin do to us?

The effect of sin on us is far greater, far more devastating and far more disastrous than most realise!

Sin results in death (Romans 6:23).

Sin results in condemnation (John 3:18).

Sin results in perdition (destruction) (Matthew 25:46).

Sin results in eternal fire (Jude verse 7).

Sin results in the lake of fire and the second death (Revelation 20:14).

Allow me to focus on one more vitally important fact. *Sin breaks our relationship with God.*

James Philip, in his booklet on repentance, says it so clearly:

Men are far too prone to think of sin (when they think of it at all) in terms of actions that are wrong or reprehensible in the eyes of society, and commonly assume that because they have not offended against common law they are therefore not sinful in the sight of God. But this is to miss the point completely. Sin is essentially a wrong relationship with God.

It may express itself in a host of ways, and indeed in some of its most serious forms, quite apart from any infringement of common law. And when the Scriptures maintain that '*there is no difference: for all have sinned and come short of the glory of God*'—they are not suggesting that all men sinned in the same way, or to the same extent, nor are they calling in question their status as law-abiding citizens. They are simply stating that in their relationship to God everything has gone wrong.

In the garden of Eden, Adam enjoyed an intimate relationship with God. It was paradise! Then he sinned! God had said:

> *Of every tree of the garden thou mayest freely eat. But of the tree of the knowledge of good and evil, thou shalt not eat of it; for in the day that thou eatest thereof thou shalt surely die.* (Genesis 2:16,17)

Did he die? He certainly did—in his relationship to God. The fellowship was gone; the relationship broken. Every one of us is born without an intimate relationship to God. This inner deadness towards God is further explained by the Apostle Paul:

> *Wherefore, as by one man sin entered into the world, and death by sin, and so death passed upon all men, for all have sinned.* (Romans 5:12)

This situation is further reinforced by each of us when we have become more entrenched into it by personally sinning, we are totally unaware of our standing before God. Sometimes we think we have a relationship, but we have none!

This is why people are so often indifferent to God's call to repentance.

To be in trouble is one thing, but to be in trouble and not know it, is even more serious. Many presume they have a relationship with God because they have Christian parents and are associated with a church, or because they have some knowledge of the Bible, and have partaken in one or other

Christian ceremony or rite. None of these things restores us to what we have lost in Adam.

We must never allow pride to rob us of honestly acknowledging that in ourselves, on the inside, we are dead towards God. Every longing in our hearts after God is something that the Holy Spirit is currently stirring up in us.

We must allow the Holy Spirit to show us the deadness of our hearts. And we must co-operate with Him, and respond to every longing for God that He generates in us afresh. Never let indifference control you.

Another reaction on the part of man to God's call to repentance is:

2. Antagonism

This person says, 'I don't want to repent!' The Holy Spirit asks an extremely relevant question through the inspired pen of the Apostle Paul:

> *Do you show contempt for the riches of his kindness, tolerance and patience, not realising that God's kindness leads you towards repentance?* (Romans 2:4 NIV)

Many react violently to the convicting call of the Spirit. God often encounters antagonism from humans. He will not do so for ever!

Sometimes the antagonism is quiet and controlled. This was the case with the rich young ruler:

> *Then Jesus beholding him loved him, and said unto him, One thing thou lackest: go thy way, sell whatever thou hast, and give to the poor and thou shalt have treasure in heaven, and come, take up the cross, and follow me. And he was sad at that saying, and went away grieved for he had great possessions.* (Mark 10:21,22)

Quiet and controlled antagonism!

Stephen was one of God's special men. When he confronted the people of his day with the truth, their reaction was violent. Stephen said to them:

> *Ye stiffnecked and uncircumcised in heart and ears, ye do always resist the Holy Spirit; as your fathers did, so do ye.*
> (Acts 7:51)

Their reaction was so violent they stoned and killed him.

That same antagonistic spirit filled the hearts of those who cried out,

> *'We will not have this man to reign over us'.*
> (Luke 19:14)

Jesus sensed this antagonism in some of the people to whom he preached. That is why he said:

> *Ye will not come to me, that ye might have life.*
> (John 5:40)

Perhaps the most frightening reaction of all to God's loving call to repentance is:

3. Incapability

For the somewhat careless person this is a sobering fact. Man is not able to repent just when he wishes to. It's like catching a wave with a surf board. If you launch yourself out in front of the wave too soon, the wave washes over you. If you move too late, you also miss the wave. Your timing is important. There is a crucial moment, and if you launch out at that moment the wave will take you right out on to the beach.

When the wave of convicting power from the Holy Spirit moves over you, that's the time to repent! Some think they can leave repenting to their dying day, but what if God sends no wave that day? That is why the Scriptures say again and again:

> Today, if you will hear his voice [ie, feel the wave of His Spirit move over you], harden not your heart.
> (Hebrews 3:7–8)

When some people sense there is something going on inside of themselves, they realise that they are not right with God. Perhaps they even feel they ought to get right with God, but somehow they don't seem to have the ability to do anything about it. This may occur several or many times during their lifetime, and yet no significant change takes place in them. The crux of the matter is that they cannot repent. Just like the man who, at the Pool of Bethesda (John 5:2–8), when the water was stirred by the angel, wanted to move into the water but was unable, so it is with repentance. Unless assisted by someone, we are incapable of repenting. Unless assisted by God, we are incapable of repenting.

Why is man plagued by this incapability? The answer to this question is not so simple, but it does underline the seriousness of sin, and the incredible grip sin has on our lives. The fact is that deep down in the back of our hearts there is a throne where self reigns. As James Philip puts it:

> Every particular sin we care to name derives its seriousness from the fact that it is the expression of this evil root. This horrible voracious thing grips all human life with vice-like power and displays that power most arrogantly when, in great weariness and despair, we most want deliverance.

Man needs supernatural help!

God supernaturally assists

At this point of desperation, God steps in to assist. He gives us the ability to repent.

Peter makes this clear:

> The God of our fathers raised up Jesus, whom ye slew and hanged on a tree. Him hath God exalted with his right hand to be a Prince and a Saviour, for to give repentance to Israel, and forgiveness of sins.

> (Acts 5:30–31)

Luke further clarifies this matter and at the same time includes the Gentiles:

> When they heard these things, they held their peace, and glorified God saying, Then hath God also to the Gentiles granted repentance unto life.
> (Acts 11:18)

How special of God not only to call us to repentance, but also to stop and supernaturally assist us!

James Philip, in his booklet on repentance, says it so beautifully:

> The miracle at Bethesda illustrates this also. When the paralytic, in response to the question, 'Wilt thou be made whole?' told Christ of his inability to move, our Lord replied with the royal command, 'Rise, take up thy bed and walk.' It was at that point that the miracle happened. The one thing that the man could not do was to rise. That had been his trouble for thirty-eight years, but the word of Christ to him was a word of power, a creative word, which bridged the gulf between the grace of God and his utter need. Grace came to him in the command to rise, and enabled him to do so. And it is with the word of the gospel and with its summons to repent. It contains within itself the power to break the

34

bondage and tyranny of indwelling sin, and bestows it as a gift of grace, enabling men to turn to God.

It is sometimes said that 'God's commands are His enablings,' and this is never so true as it is in this connection. We must never forget that the gospel is more than the story of how Christ died and rose again for our salvation. The gospel is a power, *the power of God unto salvation to everyone that believeth'*(Romans 1:16), and when the gospel is preached it unleashes a power that lays siege to men's hearts and wills, capturing them for Christ, and liberating them from the tyranny that has hitherto gripped them. As the Apostle Paul says: *it pleased God by the foolishness of preaching to save them that believe.'* (1 Corinthians 1:21).

This is a miracle, and ultimately no one can understand how it happens. As Jesus once said: *'The wind blows where it wills, and you hear the sound of it, but you do not know whence it comes or whither it goes; so it is with every one who is born of the Spirit.'* (John 3:8).

Wesley writes in one of his hymns:

> *He speaks, and listening to His voice*
> *New life the dead receive.*

What incredible power is released when God speaks! It was His word that formed the earth and all of creation. When He spoke, the storm was stilled. When He spoke, demons, disease and even death vanished. His word never falls to the ground. His word does not return to Him void—it accomplishes everything He intends it to accomplish. His word is life-giving.

Whenever that life-giving word is spoken to us, it does something in us. When He says 'Repent!' not only is He giving a command, but that command includes an enabling

to fulfil the command. This is how we are able to break
through the bondage that has held us for many years.

The other side of the coin
While it is true that without the Lord taking the initiative in
calling us to repentance and salvation, and without His
enabling us to respond, there would be no salvation, it is also
true that the Scriptures never exclude man's responsibility.
Man is able to, and does harden his heart to God's call. That
is why the Lord says:

> Today, if you will hear his voice, harden not your
> hearts.   (Hebrews 4:7)

This is the other side of the coin. God's call and man's
response make the picture complete.

The word generates faith
Our response to God's call must be a response of our faith.
But how does this work out? Well, 'every man' has been
given 'a measure of faith' (Romans 12:3), which seemingly
lies dormant in him. This measure of faith needs to be
activated. But how? For this to happen there needs to be
hearing of the word. Paul says:

> How then shall they call on him in whom they have not
> believed? And how shall they believe in him of whom
> they have not heard? And how shall they hear without a
> preacher? . . .
>   So then faith cometh by hearing, and hearing by the
> word of God.   (Romans 10:14,17)

When a person hears the word of God (hears the Lord
speak to them), that very word generates faith in them and
they are thus enabled to believe God. It's a miracle that
takes place! It is far more than a mere intellectual accept-

36

ance, although the intellect is involved. It's what Paul calls *'the hearing of faith'* (Galatians 3:2).

James Philip summarises it as follows:

> When the living truth of God touches a man's life, the 'impress' it leaves upon him is precisely this ability to obey from the heart the summons to repentance and faith in Christ.

7

The Mechanics Of Repentance

I remember a discussion I had with a very well educated man who was well into his 70s. He had recently faced the rigours of a breakup in his marriage, and he was a rather wounded man—understandably so. My contact with him had been very pleasant, and he had attended our services on a couple of occasions. He had been impressed! On this our third time together, he seemed rather delighted to tell me that he had heard one of my close friends preaching on television. I immediately asked, 'Well, what did you think of it?' He said, 'I was favourably impressed. He preaches like you—a some-what emotional preacher.' This response certainly took me by surprise. I had never rated myself an emotional preacher.

Realising that the man was not speaking disparagingly about me, I quickly asked the Holy Spirit to give me wisdom to respond to him, and almost immediately the Holy Spirit helped me.

I said to him, 'Sir, the other day I was thinking about something very important—the fact that we are made up of three parts.' I then went on to explain that we each have a body, a soul, and a spirit. I explained that our bodies relate us to the physical world; our spirits have been created in us, by God, for relationship and fellowship with Himself, and that our souls, or our personalities, play an important role in deciding whether we are going to closely relate to God, or live for the physical or material things of the world.

I then explained to him that our souls are composed of:

Our intellect
Our emotions
Our will.

He had no problems in accepting that the *will* is the most dominant part of our souls. I then suggested to him that a man's will needs to be influenced both by his intellect and emotions before it can make a valid decision to yield to God.

It was at this point that I asked him an important question: 'Sir, from what church background do you come?' He willingly shared with me that he had come from a high church background. He had attended a famous church school and he was accustomed to preachers who largely addressed the intellect. When he offered this information I began to understand where the Holy Spirit was leading me.

I then suggested that certain preachers had majored on addressing the intellect, whereas others had mainly addressed the emotions. In my way of thinking, to pursue only one of these emphases was to make an incomplete impact on the person. I suggested that only after a person's intellect had been informed by the word of God as to the fact that Jesus had died on the cross in their place, and had paid the penalty for their sin, was the way open for their emotions to be stirred by the Holy Spirit. As the Holy Spirit continued to stir such a person in their emotions, only then would there be real sorrow for sin. This understanding of the intellect and this stirring of the emotions paved the way for the will to make a decision inspired by the Holy Spirit. This would be a life-changing decision.

When I asked the gentleman, 'Sir, don't you perhaps think you were raised in an environment where your intellect was addressed to the neglect of your emotions, and thus your will has never been able to fully make the correct decision?', he responded by saying, 'You certainly have thrown light on the subject for me!'

40

Where do you stand in this matter?

May I therefore suggest that the 'mechanics' of repentance include an impact on my intellect as a result of receiving more information from, and a clearer understanding of God's word. Further to this, it involves the Holy Spirit bringing conviction on me; a realisation of my guilt before God, and consequently a sorrow for my sin. It is at this point that the Holy Spirit moves on my emotions. When both my intellect and emotions have been stirred by the Holy Spirit, my will begins to crumble and yield to Almighty God.

These are the 'mechanics' of true repentance!

8

The Ramifications Of Repentance

The tree of repentance has several major branches. Without one of the three most important branches the tree loses its symmetry.

Remorse

This branch of repentance involves a feeling of compunction or a degree of regret for a sin or a wrong committed. It is a regretful remembrance or recollection of sin or wrong. Remorse often includes tears, but tears can be present without remorse being evident. Often a person who is caught in the act of their sin will burst into tears, only to return to their sin at the next opportunity. This is particularly true, for example, of an alcoholic. Remorse, therefore, is more than tears. It involves a degree of regret that demonstrates itself in positive, corrective action. A genuinely remorseful man will turn in a positive, corrective action from the wrong that caused his remorse.

Paul makes it clear that God-given remorse or sorrow leads a person to true repentance:

> *Now I rejoice, not that you were made sorry [remorseful] but that you sorrowed to repentance; for ye were made sorry after a godly manner. For godly sorrow worketh repentance to salvation not to be repented of [or*

regretted]; but the sorrow of this world worketh death.
(2 Corinthians 7:9)

The next ramification of repentance which Jesus personally endorsed is

Restitution

This is the action of restoring or giving back to its proper owner, or of making reparation to a person for loss or injury inflicted.

It was in the city of Jericho that the little man Zacchaeus met Jesus. This encounter with Jesus released in him the God-given ability to repent. He reinforced his repentance with restitution.

> *And Zacchaeus stood, and said unto the Lord, Behold, Lord, the half of my goods I give to the poor; and if I have taken anything from any man by false accusation I restore him fourfold.* (Luke 19:8)

For this, Jesus responded by saying:

> *This day is salvation come to this house.* (verse 9)

Deeply repentant people will not only allow the Spirit of God to bring remorse on them—they will also allow the Spirit of God to lead them into acts of restitution which are clearly indicative of sincere repentance. It is the mentality that says, 'I must be completely right with God at any cost.'

Restitution needs to be handled carefully! It is not an opportunity for bringing dirty washing into the public. Perhaps a guideline that may be helpful at this stage is: Private sin—private confession (restitution); civil sin—civil con-

44

fession (restitution); public sin—public confession (restitution).

May I suggest that in pursuing restitution in your own life, you seek the guidance of your pastor, or of a mature Christian who is definitely progressing in their walk with God. This could greatly assist and protect you from being unnecessarily hurt or from hurting others in your pursuit after God.

The third ramification of repentance is:

Reformation

The first result of a person repenting is restored fellowship with Jesus. As soon as a person has come into a personal relationship with Jesus, the very character of Jesus begins to rub off on to them. For implied in the call to repentance is the call to 'Follow me'. The same Jesus who *began to preach, and to say, 'Repent; for the kingdom of heaven is at hand'* (Matthew 4:17) also said to Peter and Andrew *'Follow me'* (4:19).

Implied in the call to repentance is the call to reformation. Peter puts it this way:

> *For even hereunto were ye called: because Christ also suffered for us, leaving us an example, that ye should follow in his steps.* (1 Peter 2:21)

A person who manifests remorse and demonstrates restitution must of necessity press on to clearly exhibit reformation. To come short on any of these points is to experience a defective repentance.

Following Jesus presupposes a new way of life; a new set of values; the taking up of a new set of Christian ethics. In a word, it involves becoming a new creation.

45

9

The Christian And Repentance

Once you have entered the kingdom of heaven by way of repentance and faith, the whole kingdom lies before you, ready to be inherited. In the same way that the children of Israel crossed the Jordan and conquered territory after territory with a view to possessing the entire land, so the children of God must settle for nothing less than *all* that the Lord has promised them.

However, it's not always quite that simple. The devil is constantly on the prowl with a view to killing, stealing and destroying (John 10:10). In addition, if he can side-track us from God's perfect plan for our lives, he certainly will. He seemed to succeed in the life of the Galatian church, and that is why Paul had to write and say, *'O foolish Galatians, who hath bewitched you?'* (Galatians 3:1)

That is precisely what happened to Achan at Jericho, as recorded in the book of Joshua, chapter 7. He was side-tracked by the beautiful garment, the silver and gold. It is possible for us, in our pursuit of the Lord and His plan for our lives, to be side-tracked. This departure from God's will is sin. Whenever we sin, we, as Christians, need to repent. That is why the Lord calls on five of the seven churches in the book of the Revelation to repent. Jesus writes to the church at Ephesus and commends them on several good points, but then He says:

Remember therefore from whence thou art fallen, and

repent and do the first works [that is, repentance] *or else I will come unto thee quickly, and will remove thy lampstand out of his place, except thou repent.*

(Revelation 2:5)

The implication of these five calls to repentance is that Christians must always be willing to repent. We must never allow hardness of heart, based on pride, to stop us from repenting. As soon as we contravene God's law, or move slightly out of the centre of His will, and the Holy Spirit brings the restlessness of conviction on us, we must repent immediately. We must keep short accounts with God.

Repentance, therefore, is not a once-for-all happening at the time of our conversion. It is an on-going response to the Holy Spirit, resulting in a life of constant fellowship with the Lord. Repentance brings us into the family of God and it also keeps us in an intimate relationship with the Father.

10

Personal Application

The most important aspect of this teaching now comes into focus. Don't stop reading now! You might miss a blessing.

Have you ever travelled the roadway of repentance? If you will give the Holy Spirit an opportunity, He will walk with you all the way along this road. In the process He will first of all show you yourself, and then He will show you Jesus.

R. A. Torrey tells a never-to-be-forgotten story in this regard in his book, *The Holy Spirit, Who He is and What He Does*.

The story is told of a faithful Scottish minister who was travelling through Scotland and stopped one night at an inn. The innkeeper came to him and asked him if he would conduct family worship. He replied that he would if the innkeeper on his part would bring to the worship all the guests in the house, and all the servants. This the innkeeper agreed to do. When they were gathered in the big room for the service the minister turned to the innkeeper and said, 'Are all the servants here?' 'Yes,' replied the innkeeper. 'All?' persisted the minister. 'Well, not all. All but one. There is one girl who works down in the kitchen washing the pots and kettles, who is so dirty that she is not fit to come to the meeting.' The minister replied, 'We will not go on with the service until she comes.' He insisted and the innkeeper went for this servant and brought her in. This faithful man of God became greatly interested in this poor, neglected creature; and when the others were passing out of the room he asked her if she would not stay for a few minutes. And when everyone had gone he said to her, 'I want to teach you a prayer for you to offer: "Lord, show me myself". Will you offer it every day?' She replied that she would. The next day the minister left, but a short time afterwards came back again and asked the innkeeper about this girl. The innkeeper replied, 'She is spoiled, she is no good at all. She is weeping all the time, weeping day and night, and can hardly attend to her work.' The minister asked to see her again, and when she came in the minister said, 'Now I want to teach you another prayer, "Lord, show me Thyself." Now pray that prayer every day.'

The minister left and a few years afterwards was preaching one Lord's day morning in a church in Glasgow. At the close of the service a neat, trim-looking young woman came up to him and said, 'Do you recognise me?' He replied, 'No, I do not.' She said, 'Do you recall holding a service in an inn and speaking to one of the servants afterwards and teaching her to pray the prayer, "Lord, show me myself", and afterwards teaching her the other prayer, "Lord, show me Thyself?" 'Oh, yes,' he said, 'I remember that.' 'Well,' she said, 'I am that girl. And when you taught me that first prayer and went away, and I asked God to show me myself, He gave me such a view of my vileness and my sin that I was overwhelmed with grief and could scarcely sleep at night or work by day for thinking of my sins.' 'Then,' she said, 'when you came back and taught me the second prayer, "Lord, show me Thyself", God gave me such a view of Himself, of His love and of Jesus Christ dying on the cross for me, that all the burden of my sin rolled away and I became a happy Christian.'

Yes, those are the two things that each of us needs to see—our own sin, and it is the work of the Holy Spirit to show us that, and the righteousness of Christ and the righteousness that God has provided for you and me in Jesus Christ, and it is the work of the Holy Spirit to show us that also.

11

The Steps Into Repentance

In order to experience real Holy Spirit-inspired repentance, it is vitally important to allow the Holy Spirit *time*. Time to show us our sins. Time to show us ourselves. Time to show us our desperate need of Jesus. Time to show us that Jesus is able to meet our every need. This involves being still, sitting quietly and contemplatively before the Lord, and allowing the Holy Spirit to do the thorough work He is wanting to do.

Would you consider allowing God enough time to do this work in you? Would you? If so, may I suggest that you:

Take these steps

Set a specific time aside. Take the morning off. Take the day off. Set the evening aside. Get alone with God. Go to a place where you will not be disturbed. Mean business with God.

When you are alone with the Lord, give the Holy Spirit time. Turn to the pages of this booklet that deal with the *need* for repentance, and let the Spirit of God begin to show you the effect that sin has had on you, remembering that this is God's view of the effect of sin on each one of us. Then turn to the section that deals with the *call* to repentance, and prayerfully read the Scripture references. Remember, this is God's call to you—His loving call.

Then turn to the section that explains the *meaning* of

repentance, and let the Holy Spirit prepare you for this right-about turn.

As you now turn to the section that deals with the *nature* of repentance, you come to some of the most important steps that can ever be taken by a person seeking after God.

The step of confession

As you sit quietly in the presence of the Holy Spirit, allow Him to put His spotlight on every area of your life, present and past. The moment any area of sin and hardness, or resentment, comes into focus, immediately confess it as sin before God. Make this confession audibly. Let this process continue. The Holy Spirit is faithful. He will bring into focus all that needs to be brought into focus. Once you have dealt with each area, accept the fact that *all* is now confessed.

The step of repentance

Now tell the Lord you are turning your back on every sin you have confessed. Say it out loud. 'Lord, with the help of your Spirit and by your grace, I now turn my back on all the sins I have confessed. I repent of them. I now start a new way of living. I truly repent of all my wickedness.'

The step of repentance from dead works

Ponder a while over the dead works you have relied on— your Christian background—your church affiliation—your knowledge of the Bible. Think on the other things you have tried to rely on as a basis of salvation. Repent of them:

Lord, I repent of all my dead works. (Name them

before the Lord.) Forgive me for relying on any of these hollow forms. Lord, I now rely on you *alone*; on your blood shed for my forgiveness; on your death on the cross in my place. You are my salvation—my Saviour. I accept this as a fact and thank you from the depths of my heart. I praise you, Lord, for what you have done for me, and in me. Thank you that you have supernaturally assisted me.

The step of receiving

'I now invite you to become the Lord and king of my life. Come and live in me. I am available to you.'
John 1:12 says:

> *But as many as received him, to them gave he power to become the sons of God, even to them that believe in his name.*

Revelation 3:20 says:

> *Behold, I stand at the door and knock; if any man hear my voice, and open the door, I will come in to him, and will sup with him, and he with me.*

Meditate on these verses as long as you like, asking the question, 'Now that I have taken these steps, what does God say in His Word that He has done for me?' Give the Holy Spirit time to bring these verses alive to you.

The step of recognising

Carefully note 1 John 5:11–13:

> *And this is the record, that God hath given to us eternal*

life, and this life is in his Son. He that hath the Son hath life; and he that hath not the Son, hath not life. (verse 11)

These things have I written unto you that believe on the name of the son of God that ye may know that ye have eternal life... (verse 13)

Then say to the Lord:

Lord, thank you that when I received you, you came in to live in me. I recognise this is a fact. Thank you, too, that because eternal life is in you, when you came to live in me, you gave me yourself and eternal life. I recognise that I have you living in me and therefore I have eternal life in me. Thank you that you have said: *'I will never leave you nor forsake you'* (Hebrews 13:5). I recognise that I am yours and you are mine. Thank you.

❖ ❖ ❖ ❖